First World War
and Army of Occupation
War Diary
France, Belgium and Germany

56 DIVISION
169 Infantry Brigade,
Brigade Trench Mortar Battery
2 March 1916 - 28 August 1916

WO95/2963/4

The Naval & Military Press Ltd
www.nmarchive.com
Published in association with The National Archives

Published by

The Naval & Military Press Ltd

Unit 10 Ridgewood Industrial Park,

Uckfield, East Sussex,

TN22 5QE England

Tel: +44 (0) 1825 749494

www.naval-military-press.com

www.nmarchive.com

This diary has been reprinted in facsimile from the original. Any imperfections are inevitably reproduced and the quality may fall short of modern type and cartographic standards.

© **Crown Copyright**
Images reproduced by permission of The National Archives, London, England, 2015.

Contents

Document type	Place/Title	Date From	Date To
Heading	WO95/2963/4 1916 Mar-Aug Brigade Trench Mortar Compy		
Heading	56 Div 169 Bde 169 Trench Mortar Bty 1916 Mar To 1916 Aug		
Heading	War Diary Of 169/1 T.M.B. From March To May 1916 Vol 1,2,3		
War Diary		02/03/1916	02/03/1916
War Diary	Houvin	03/04/1916	23/05/1916
War Diary	Hebuterne	25/05/1916	25/05/1916
War Diary	Houvin	06/05/1916	06/05/1916
War Diary	Halloy	07/05/1916	07/05/1916
War Diary	Souastre	20/05/1916	20/05/1916
War Diary	Sailly	21/05/1916	21/05/1916
War Diary	Hebuterne	22/05/1916	21/06/1916
War Diary	Halloy	24/06/1916	24/06/1916
War Diary	Hebuterne	24/06/1916	28/06/1916
War Diary	Souastre	30/06/1916	30/06/1916
War Diary	Hebuterne	01/07/1916	02/07/1916
War Diary	Bayencourt	03/07/1916	03/07/1916
War Diary	St Amand	06/07/1916	06/07/1916
War Diary	Fonquevillers	07/07/1916	08/07/1916
War Diary	Souastre	12/07/1916	22/07/1916
War Diary	Hannescamps	24/07/1916	30/07/1916
Miscellaneous	Appendices		
Map	Map		
Heading	169th Brigade 56th Division 169th Light Trench Mortar Battery August 1916		
War Diary	Hannescamps	01/08/1916	19/08/1916
War Diary	St Amand	20/08/1916	20/08/1916
War Diary	Sus St Leger	22/08/1916	22/08/1916
War Diary	Maizicourt	23/08/1916	23/08/1916
War Diary	Agenvillers	25/08/1916	28/08/1916
Heading	1/16 London Regt Vol XVII		
Heading	1/16 London Regt Vol XVI		

WO 95/2963/4

1916 Mar - Aug.

Brigade Trench Mortar Comp'y.

56 DIV
169 BDE

169
TRENCH MORTAR BTY
1916 MAR to 1916 Aug

2826

War Diary
169/1 7 T.M.B
from March to May 1916

LVI

Vol 1 2 3

Leibl Nathan
Lieut
O.C
169/1 7 T.M.B

31.V.16

Army Form C. 2118.

WAR DIARY
or
INTELLIGENCE SUMMARY
(Erase heading not required.)

Instructions regarding War Diaries and Intelligence Summaries are contained in F. S. Regs., Part II. and the Staff Manual respectively. Title Pages will be prepared in manuscript.

Place	Date	Hour	Summary of Events and Information	Remarks and references to Appendices
	2/III/16		Battery joined 2/III/16 from L.R.B. and 2 V.R. Trained at T.M. School at VALHEUREUX.	
		1.30 P.M	Arrived GOREN FLOS. 8/III/16	
		2.30 P.M	" FIENVILLERS. 12/III/16	
		4. P.M	" DOULLENS 15/III/16	
		4.15 P.M	" HOUVIN 16/III/16	
			The Brigadier inspected the Battery at Drill 14/III/16	

Army Form C. 2118.

WAR DIARY
or
INTELLIGENCE SUMMARY
(Erase heading not required.)

Place	Date	Hour	Summary of Events and Information	Remarks and references to Appendices
HOUVIN	3/IV/16	10.30 A.M	A demonstration took place in the Brigade. 200 men from each Battalion were present, and as many officers as possible from the Brigade.	

Scheme

The general idea was to demonstrate the "noise proof" of the Stokes gun – and to show that a Barrage of pure could be erected.

A platoon of Infantry assisted and open the given signal they went into an opposing enemy position while rapid fire was poured advanced 90 yds & 32 Bombs were used – 2 of which failed to explode by the Battalion. The demonstration was held to be very successful by the Brigadier.

The remainder of the week was passed in routine work

Army Form C. 2118

WAR DIARY
or
INTELLIGENCE SUMMARY

(Erase heading not required.)

Instructions regarding War Diaries and Intelligence Summaries are contained in F. S. Regs., Part II. and the Staff Manual respectively. Title Pages will be prepared in manuscript.

Place	Date	Hour	Summary of Events and Information	Remarks and references to Appendices
	22/4/16		The Battery was detailed from the 1st Battalion Queens Westminster Rifles and 1st Bn Q.W. London Regiment R.F. and marched to the Third Army French Mortar School at Hugny de Flochille	
	30/4/16	10.30 am	The Battery rejoined the Brigade at HOUVIN-HOUVIGNEUL by route march	
	7/5/16	11.30 am	Marched to HALLOY	
	20/5/16	7 p.m.	Marched to SOUASTRE + relieved the 168/2 T.M.B.	
	21/5/16	2.00 p.m.	Marched to SAILLY-LE-BOIS — being relieved by 168/2 T.M.B.	
	22/5/16	2.30 pm	Marched to HEBUTERNE + took over from 167/2 T.M.B.	
	23/5/16	5.0 p.m.	Four Mortars drawn from D.A.D.O.S. Stores	
HEBUTERNE	26/5/16	7.0 pm	Conference with Brigade Major + received orders not to continue emplacement work begun by 167/2 T.M.B. but to attend by pinning completion of new trenches	

Army Form C. 2118.

WAR DIARY
or
INTELLIGENCE SUMMARY
(Erase heading not required.)

Instructions regarding War Diaries and Intelligence Summaries are contained in F. S. Regs., Part II. and the Staff Manual respectively. Title Pages will be prepared in manuscript.

Place	Date	Hour	Summary of Events and Information	Remarks and references to Appendices
HOUVIN	6/V/16	9 A.M.	The Battery moved to HALLOY	
HALLOY	7/V/16		" " SOUASTRE 20/V/16	
SOUASTRE	20/V/16		" " SAILLY 21/V/16	
SAILLY	21/V/16		" " HEBUTERNE 22/V/16	
HEBUTERNE	22/V/16			
			Two guns were dug in to at to is a position to fire on our own front line in the event of its being occupied by the enemy. Last place was removed on 25/V/16 after a conference with the Bgd. Engr.	
			N.B. The distance between the Trenches was too great to allow any offensive fire	

Army Form C. 2118.

169 TMB

WAR DIARY or INTELLIGENCE SUMMARY

(Erase heading not required.)

Place	Date	Hour	Summary of Events and Information	Remarks and references to Appendices
HEBUTERNE	14.6.16		Trench Mortar Batteries 169/1 and 169/2 were merged into 169 Trench Mortar Battery under command of Lt P.C. COOTE who was promoted to Captain on assuming command. The other officers were Lt G.G. NATHAN R.E.R. WILLIAMSON & 2nd Lt J.B. PITTMAN.	
HEBUTERNE	15/16/17/18.6.16	night	Built new dug outs in the Bryan de Lisses either side of Yiddish Star & Yellow Street.	
- do -	15.6.16	day	50% Personnel joined including 2nd Lt R.G.T GROVES	
- do -	19.6.16		One of the four dug outs in the Bryan de Lisses blown in by shell fire. Moved 1560 rounds of 3" Stokes Ammunition into the recess after detonation with 11 second fuse and green cartridge. Also detonated 480 rounds with same fuse and cartridge, which were left at the Brigade Stokes Ammunition dump.	
- do -	21.6.16		Moved to HALLOY joined by 167 Trench Mortar Battery. No I Section.	

2449 Wt. W14957/M90 750,000 1/16 J.B.C. & A. Forms/C.2118/12.

WAR DIARY
or
INTELLIGENCE SUMMARY

Army Form C. 2118.

Place	Date	Hour	Summary of Events and Information	Remarks and references to Appendices
HALLOY	24.6.16		Moved to HEBUTERNE and reported to 169' Brigade, leaving Lt. H.G.T. RICKS behind sick.	
HEBUTERNE	24.6.16		Received orders to cut down enemy wire with Mortar fire in accordance with attached Memo. As only Section 7 of 169 Trench Mortar Battery and a few of 169 Trench Mortar Battery had arrived, emplacements had to be dug. The Brigade gave the O/C instructions to get two emplacements prepared next night, with a view to firing at 9.45 am on 26th JUNE.	No 1.
"	25.6.16		Captain COOTE & Lieutant WALLACE (officers commanding 169 TMB & Z 36 Medium TMB) reconnoitered the Royan de Oliviere between Yankee and Yellow streets. Two points were chosen on the Royan de Oliviere, one midway between Yankee street and the communication trench leading to the front line, one to the rear of this communication trench & the other between Yellow street & the communication trench. A fatigue of 40 men were provided and under Lt EATA LANE prepared these emplacements and an ammunition recess during the night 25-26 June.	

WAR DIARY
or
INTELLIGENCE SUMMARY

(Erase heading not required.)

Army Form C. 2118.

Place	Date	Hour	Summary of Events and Information	Remarks and references to Appendices
HEBUTERNE	26.6.16		As working party, details by the Brigade Major carried up 250 rounds of Stoke's ammunition and at 9.45 a.m. three mortars were fired during an enemy bombardment of only 3 minutes duration. Lieut. NATHAN directed the fire while Captain COOTE & Sergeant BROOKS observed the direction of fire from the head of the communication trench in the front line. At 10.15 a.m. smoke was sent over and the enemy retaliated by shelling the front line, communication trenches, and village. At 10 a.m. No 3 gun had been sent off as the base plate had sunk badly and Nos. 1 and 2, on finishing their ammunition retired into a dug out on the Serjeant de Louvre. Captain COOTE, Lt NATHAN, Sergt BROOKS and two gunners made their way down the communication trench and meeting some of No 3 gun coming back from the village, the village being shelled very heavily, they all retired into a dug out in Yellow Street when the enemy guns ceased firing, they returned to their billets. Later four 5.9 shells fell into the yard of the Officers Mess & killed ? PRICE and six men and wounded ten men of the Section of 167 T.M.B	

WAR DIARY
or
INTELLIGENCE SUMMARY
(Erase heading not required.)

Army Form C. 21

Place	Date	Hour	Summary of Events and Information	Remarks and references to Appendices
HEBUTERNE	26.6.16 (cont)		attached to the Battery. Later Lt NATHAN went into Hospital with shell shock. Later on in the day the Brigadier gave orders for the Trench Mortar Battery not to fire the remainder of their programme and for it to attach's rations of 1 by T.M.B. to continue firing emplacements on XHQ in order to fire two rounds before Zero (see telegram 10)	No. 2
-do-	27.6.16		Captain COOTE received orders to meet Brigade Major at ST AMAND where he received final orders for the attack from the Brigade O.F.R., O.W.R., and L'R.B.	
-do-	28.6.16		Captain COOTE returned to HEBUTERNE and received a telegram to say that the operations had been postponed ?? 48 hours. (RO1G) orders were given to proceed to SOUASTRE	
SOUASTRE	30.6.16	midnight 10 p.m.	Moved to SOUASTRE at 10 p.m. 10 QVR, 10 L.R.B., 1 20 OWR reported as carriers at 8 pm. Men were given a 25 min run from London & report at 11.30 a.m. Glentworth. Battery Transport moved to Hebuterne at 10½ a.m. b. 1st route.	No 3

J. B. Coote. Capt. 1/16 TMB

Army Form C. 2113.

WAR DIARY
or
INTELLIGENCE SUMMARY

(Erase heading not required.)

Instructions regarding War Diaries and Intelligence Summaries are contained in F. S. Regs., Part II. and the Staff Manual respectively. Title Pages will be prepared in manuscript.

Place	Date	Hour	Summary of Events and Information	Remarks and references to Appendices
			Appendices:-	
			N° 1. Copy of Orders for Wire-cutting	
			N° 2. Copy of Telegram cancelling orders for wire-cutting	
			N° 3. Description of Red Route.	
			J. Frost. Capt.	

WAR DIARY
INTELLIGENCE SUMMARY

169 TMB'y
Fol 3

Place	Date	Hour	Summary of Events and Information	Remarks and references to Appendices
HEBUTERNE	July 1	1.30 a.m.	Battery, with ammunition carriers attached, took up their positions as detailed in orders. The Head Quarters of the battery was at Billet 280, where the 50% reserve also remained, vide Telegram No I S.C. 169. Captain Oliver O/C No I Section 169 Trench Mortar Battery reported to Captain Cooke that he was unable to rise from the front of L as previously ordered for two minutes before ZERO, and that his men were in their billets in the KEEP. He remained at Billet 280 for orders.	No I No. III III
		2.30 a.m.	Captain Cooke reported to Brigade that the battery had proceeded to assembly positions.	
		9.30 a.m.	Corporal Wright and Rifleman Golding of Nos 7 & 8 Mortars reported that they were unable to get Mortars across to the German line. Lance Corporal Wells of No. 7 Mortar, reported separation of parts and he was unable to find his mortar.	

Army Form C. 2118.

WAR DIARY
or
INTELLIGENCE SUMMARY
(Erase heading not required.)

Place	Date	Hour	Summary of Events and Information	Remarks and references to Appendices
HEBUTERNE	July 1.	7.45 am	Sent a party under Sergeant Hill consisting of 6 men. 1 corporal of No.1 Section 167 T.M.B. and Rifleman Hyde with four men from the same section to the dumps in the BOYAU to detonate ammunition.	
		8.30 am	Rfn. Hyde's party returned most of them suffering from dull shock. Sergeant Hill's party returned after detonating 100 rounds.	
		11.30 am	Lieut GROVES took the same party to the Brigade Dumps and detonated a further supply which was taken No: IV up to the trenches placed in the BOYAU. The barrage being too severe to enable any being taken across.	
		4 pm	3911 Pte PETTY.S. (2nd LONDON Reg.) reported carrying mortar to German front line. Rfn. HOLLINGHAM. N.O.5 mortar reported returning with mounting. Rfn. FOULSER. No.3 mortar reported LIEUT. LANE, wounded and the battery retiring	2

WAR DIARY or INTELLIGENCE SUMMARY

Army Form C. 2118.

Place	Date	Hour	Summary of Events and Information	Remarks and references to Appendices
HEBUTERNE	July 1.	9 p.m.	Corporal BEDWORTH reported loss of No 2. Team and Mortars.	
		11.5 p.m.	Rifleman DREBLOW reported returning with LIEUT. LANE'S section to leave the German lines and he also reported that LIEUT. WILLIAMSON was in our front line in charge of a Lewis Gun. Reported this to Brigade and on instructions received from Brigade, ordered LIEUT. WILLIAMSON to return to Head Quarters and report.	
	July 2.	4.30 p.m.	Moved to BAYENCOURT, via SAILLY AU BOIS. Rifleman 2738 Barnes S.J. and Rifleman 4091 Oakes J. wounded by shell in street at 8 p.m. Barnes, since died of wounds.	
BAYENCOURT	July 3.	3.30 p.m.	Moved to ST AMAND	
ST AMAND	July 6.	9 A.m.	Moved to FONQUEVILLERS	
FONQUEVILLERS	?		Captain COOTE, Officer Commanding Battery, went to Divisional Rest Station, MONDICOURT	
"	"	6.30 p.m.	Moved to SOUASTRE	
SOUASTRE	"		Captain COOTE returned from Divisional Rest Station.	

3

WAR DIARY
or
INTELLIGENCE SUMMARY

(Erase heading not required.)

Army Form C. 2118.

Place	Date	Hour	Summary of Events and Information	Remarks and references to Appendices
SOUASTRE	July 20.		Captain COOTE, on instructions received from Brigade reported to Brigade at BIENVILLERS & reconnoitred position for emplacement, on extreme left of Brigade line.	
	21.		Captain COOTE, saw O/c 2/2 Field Coy. R.E. and made arrangements for tunneling dugouts & making emplacements for billeting	
			Lieut. WILLIAMSON proceeded to HANNESCAMPS.	
	22.	9.30 p.m.	Battery moved to HANNESCAMPS.	
HANNES-CAMPS	24.		Captain Munro 1/2 London Field Coy. R.E. reconnoitred with Captain Coote for a mined dugout behind the junction of 744/745.	
		10 p.m.	Lieuts. Williamson & Groves reconnoitred for an O.P.	
	27.		mined dugout behind 2 y4 & 2 y5.	
			Started mining on position chosen, under superintendence of H. Sappers of 2/2 London Field Coy. R.E.	

WAR DIARY
or
INTELLIGENCE SUMMARY

(Erase heading not required.)

Army Form C. 2118.

Place	Date	Hour	Summary of Events and Information	Remarks and references to Appendices
HANNESCAMPS.	July 28	10 am	Captain Cooke reconnoitred position behind Z 24 for defensive positions.	
		8.30 am	4 Sappers were titched with the battery for the Letter carrying on of the work.	
	30.	7.30 pm	13 men joined the battery after course at French Mortar School to complete establishment.	

July 31st 1918.

J. Scott
Captain
O/C 169 T.M.B.

WAR DIARY
or
INTELLIGENCE SUMMARY

(Erase heading not required.)

Army Form C. 2118.

APPENDICES

1. Copy of Staff Captain's telegram.
2. Copy of Brigade Major's telegram.
3. Copy of O.C. 169 T.M.B.'s orders to T.M.B. 4 N.U.B.
4. Copy of O.C. 169 T.M.B.'s orders to LIEUTS PITTMAN, LANE, WILLIAMSON, GROVES
5. Copy of map of German positions & entrenchments
6. Copy of O.C. 169 T.M.B.'s report on operations of the battery
7. List of Casualties incurred in action on July 1st.

J. F. Short
Captain.
O/c 169 T.M.B.

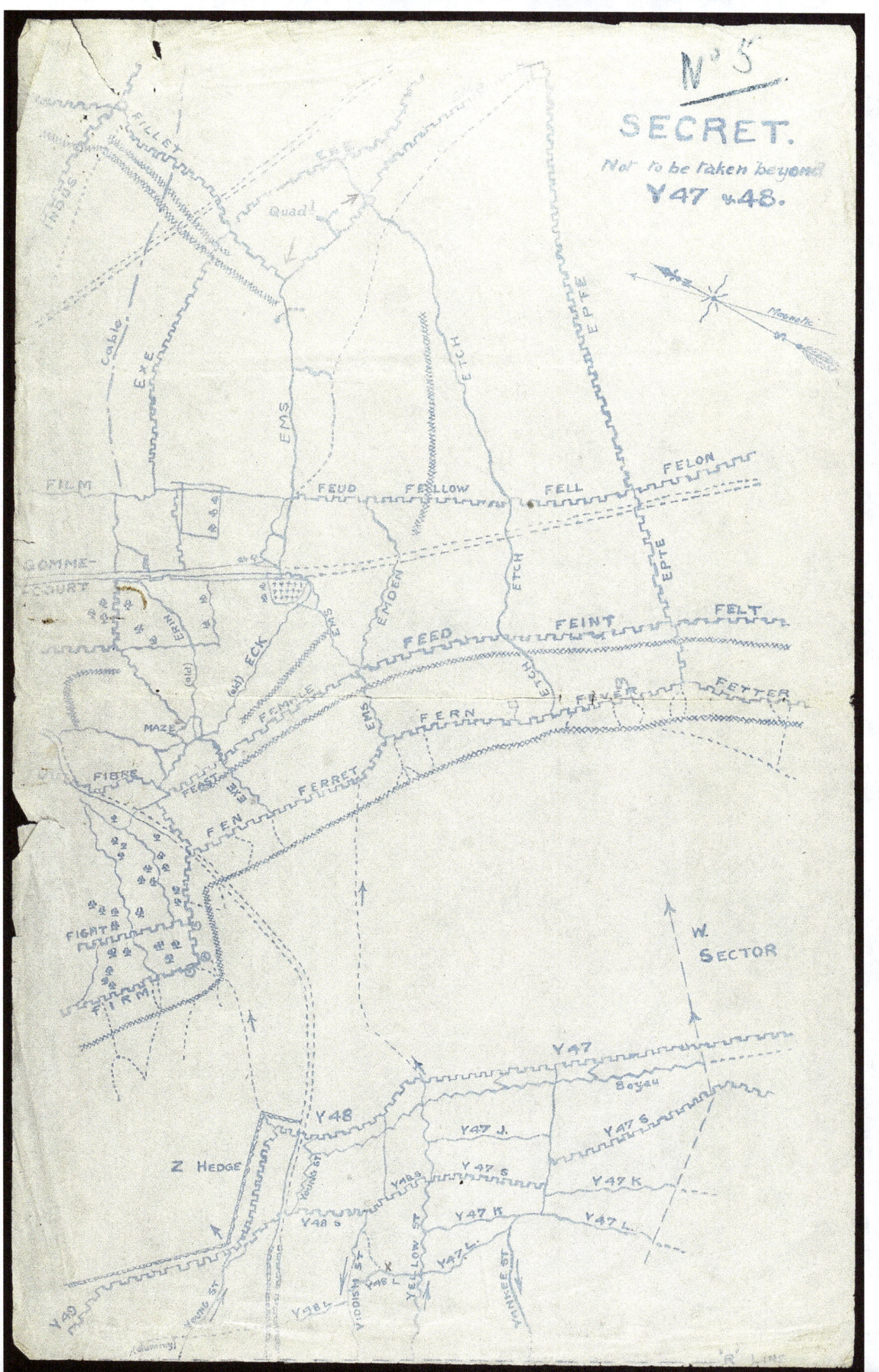

169th Brigade/
56th Division.

169th LIGHT TRENCH MORTAR BATTERY

AUGUST 1 9 1 6 ::

WAR DIARY
or
INTELLIGENCE SUMMARY
(Erase heading not required.)

Army Form C. 2118

169 TM Bty

Vol 6

Place	Date	Hour	Summary of Events and Information	Remarks and references to Appendices
HANNESCAMPS	1.8.16		2/Lieut W.H. SENDALL reported, vice Lieut G.G. NATHAN.	
	3.8.16		2/Lieut R.G.T. GROVES went down sick.	
	9.8.16		Bombardment of enemy saps by battery fire. (see addenda)	1
	13.8.16		Lieut E.R. WILLIAMSON reconnoitred position for emplacements in ROBERTS AVENUE.	
	14.8.16		Head Quarters in HANNESCAMPS heavily shelled. Six direct hits on roof of dug-out.	
			Casualties :- NIL	
			Damage :- Three handcarts rendered unserviceable.	
	17.8.16		Stokes Gun" dump established in ROBERTS AVENUE.	
	19.8.16		Relief by 57th T.M.B at 3pm March to St AMAND. Captain P.C. COOTE returned to duty.	
St AMAND	20.8.16		Left St AMAND at 2pm March to SdS St LEGER.	
SdS St LEGER	22.8.16		Left SdS St LEGER at 6.15 am. March to MAIZICOURT.	
MAIZICOURT	23.8.16		Left MAIZICOURT at 8.30 am. March to AGENVILLERS.	
AGENVILLERS	25.8.16		Captain P.C. COOTE went sick.	
	26.8.16		2/Lieut A.T. WHITTLE reported.	
	26.8.16		Captain P.C. COOTE returns to duty.	

J.B. Brooke
Captain
O/C 169 T.M.B.
31/8/16

56

1/16 London Regt

Vol XVII

56

1/16 London Regt

Vol XVI

www.ingramcontent.com/pod-product-compliance
Lightning Source LLC
Chambersburg PA
CBHW081506160426
43193CB00014B/2609